A Textual Key to the New Testament
A list of Omissions and Changes

copyright © 1993, 2002 Trinitarian Bible Society
G. W. Anderson

A Textual Key to the New Testament

A list of Omissions and Changes
by G.W. and D.E. Anderson

In recent years, much has been said and written regarding the excellence, accuracy and readability of the modern versions of the New Testament. It is often stated that these versions are more accurate than the Authorised (King James) Version because the newer translations are based upon older and better manuscripts than those upon which the Authorised Version is based. There are many today, however, who would not agree with this assessment. It is their contention that the manuscripts of the New Testament used in the modern versions are corrupted and, in effect, detract from essential doctrines of the Bible. The Trinitarian Bible Society has provided the list below as a useful guide in opposing the use of these manuscripts and modern translations.

The list below is a compilation of verses in which the modern versions have followed corrupted manuscripts and made drastic alterations to the traditionally accepted text of the New Testament. The central purpose of this list is to aid the Bible student in discerning and evaluating whether his translation is founded upon these few 'older' manuscripts, and how far astray his translation goes. A simple comparison of the verses below with any modern translation will show the extent of corruption in our modern versions.

The comparison of these modern versions needs to be made by using a copy of the Authorised Version. While perfection is not claimed for the Authorised Version or for any other version, it is an accurate and excellent translation which follows the Traditional or Received Text of the New Testament and was not affected by the current rage of paraphrasing. Some versions will be difficult to compare because of the modern tendency among translators to use 'dynamic equivalence' methods of translation (see the *New International Version: What today's Christian needs to know about the NIV*, published by the Society).

This list of variant readings is not complete. It is designed to show the many and most serious omissions in the modern editions of the New Testament. In addition to omissions, a few instances of change and additions are included. Unless otherwise stated, each variant listed represents an omission.

It is hoped that many will see the problems with the modern texts and versions and will change back to a 'complete' edition of the New Testament. It is the prayer of the Trinitarian Bible Society that God will be pleased to use this textual variant list to call His people back to a day of purer translations and sounder principles of translation and textual criticism.

A List of Omissions and Changes
Found in Most Modern New Testaments

Unless otherwise noted, the variant listed represents an omission from the Traditional Text.

An asterisk indicates some of the more serious omissions or doctrinal problems. In instances of change, the Authorised Version reading, which represents the reading of the Traditional Text, is given in comparison with the critical text reading as found in the New American Standard Version.

MATTHEW

1.7	'Asa' is changed to 'Asaph' [often this error is printed in the margin rather than in the text]
1.10	'Amon' is changed to 'Amos' [see verse 7 above]
*1.25	'firstborn'
*4.12	'Jesus'
*4.18	'Jesus'
*4.23	'Jesus'
5.22	'without a cause'
5.27	'by them of old time'
*5.44	'bless them that curse you, do good to them that hate you,' and 'despitefully use you, and'
5.47	'publicans' is changed to 'Gentiles'
6.4	'openly'
6.6	'openly'
6.13	'For thine…Amen'
6.18	'openly'
*6.33	AV–'the kingdom of God'; NAS–'His kingdom'
*8.3	'Jesus'
*8.5	'Jesus'
*8.7	'Jesus'
8.15	'them' is changed to 'him'
*8.29	'Jesus' ['Jesus, thou Son of God']
8.31	'suffer us to go away' is changed to 'send us'
9.8	'they marvelled' is changed to 'they were afraid' [RSV; NAS–'they were filled with awe']
*9.12	'Jesus'
9.13	'to repentance'
9.14	'oft'
9.35	'among the people'
9.36	'fainted' is changed to 'distressed'
10.3	'Lebbaeus, whose surname was'
11.2	'two of his disciples' is changed to 'by his disciples'
12.8	'even'
12.15	'multitudes'
12.22	'blind and' [second instance]
*12.25	'Jesus'
12.35	'of the heart'
*13.36	'Jesus'
*13.51	'Jesus saith unto them'
*13.51	'Lord' ['Yea, Lord']
*14.14	'Jesus'
*14.22	'Jesus'
*14.25	'Jesus'
14.30	'boisterous'
14.33	'came and'

2

Matthew

15.6	'or his mother'		baptism that I am baptized with:' [see also verse 22]
15.6	'commandment' is changed to 'word'	21.4	AV–'All this'; NAS–'now this'
15.8	'draweth nigh unto me with their mouth, and'	21.12	'of God' ['the temple of God']
		21.44	ALL of this verse is omitted in some versions
15.16	'Jesus'	22.13	'take him away, and'
* 15.30	'Jesus'	22.30	'of God' ['angels of God']
16.3	'O *ye* hypocrites'	* 22.37	'Jesus'
16.4	'the prophet'	23.3	AV–'they bid you observe, *that* observe and do'; NAS–'they tell you, do and observe'
* 16.20	'Jesus'		
17.4	'Let us make' is changed to 'I will make'		
17.11	AV–'Jesus'; NAS–'He'	* 23.8	'*even* Christ'
17.11	'unto them'	23.14	ALL OF THIS VERSE IS OMITTED
17.11	'first' ['shall first come']		
* 17.20	'Jesus'	* 24.2	'Jesus'
* 17.21	ALL OF THIS VERSE IS OMITTED	24.6	'all' ['all *these things*']
		24.7	'and pestilences'
17.22	'abode' is changed to 'were gathering together'	24.36	'nor the Son' is added
		24.42	'hour' is changed to 'day'
* 18.2	'Jesus'	24.48	'his coming'
* 18.11	ALL OF THIS VERSE IS OMITTED	25.6	'cometh'
		25.13	'wherein the Son of man cometh'
18.29	'at his feet'		
18.29	'all' ['I will pay thee all']	25.31	'holy' ['holy angels']
18.35	'their trespasses'	25.44	'him' ['answer him']
* 19.9	'and whoso marrieth her which is put away doth commit adultery.'	26.3	'and the scribes'
		* 26.28	'new' ['of the new testament']
		26.59	'and elders'
19.17	AV–'*there is* none good but one, *that is*, God'; NAS–'there is *only* One who is good'	26.60	'*yet* found they none' [second instance]
		26.60	'false witnesses' [second instance]
		27.2	'Pontius'
19.20	'from my youth up'	* 27.24	'just' [AV–'the blood of this just person'; NAS –'this Man's blood']
19.29	'or wife'		
20.7	'and whatsoever is right, *that* shall ye receive'		
		27.34	AV–'vinegar', i.e., sour wine; NAS–'wine'
20.16	'for many be called, but few chosen'		
		* 27.35	'that it…lots' [last half of the verse is omitted]
* 20.22	'and to be baptized with the baptism that I am baptized with?' [see also verse 23]		
* 20.23	'and be baptised with the		

3

27.42	'if' [AV–'If he be the King'; NAS–'He is the King']	6.16	'from the dead'
27.42	'believe him' is changed to 'believe in him'	6.33	'him' is changed to 'them'
		6.33	'and came together unto him'
27.64	'by night'	*6.34	'Jesus'
28.2	'from the door'	6.36	AV–'buy themselves bread: for they have nothing to eat'; NAS –'buy themselves something to eat'
28.9	'as they went to tell his disciples'		
28.20	'Amen'	6.44	'about' [AV–'about five thousand']

MARK

		7.2	'they found fault'
		*7.8	'*as* the washing…ye do' [last half of the verse is omitted]
*1.1	'the Son of God' [omitted in some versions and margins]	*7.16	ALL OF THIS VERSE IS OMITTED
*1.2	'the prophets' is replaced by 'Isaiah the prophet', an obvious error	7.24	'and Sidon'
		*7.27	'Jesus'
*1.14	'of the kingdom' [AV–'the gospel of the kingdom of God'; NAS –'the gospel of God']	*8.1	'Jesus'
		*8.17	'Jesus'
		8.17	'yet' [AV–'have ye your heart yet hardened?']
*1.41	'Jesus'	8.25	'made him look up' is changed to 'looked intently'
2.2	'straightway'		
*2.17	'to repentance'	8.26	'neither' and 'nor' are combined into 'not'
3.5	'whole as the other'		
3.15	'to heal sicknesses, and'	*9.24	'Lord' [referring to Jesus]
3.16	'And He appointed the twelve:' is added at beginning of the verse	*9.29	'and fasting'
		*9.42	'in me'
		*9.44	ALL OF THIS VERSE IS OMITTED
3.29	'damnation' is changed to 'sin'		
4.4	'of the air'	*9.45	'into the fire that never shall be quenched'
4.9	'unto them'		
*5.13	'Jesus' is changed to 'he'	*9.46	ALL OF THIS VERSE IS OMITTED
*5.19	'Jesus'		
6.11	'whosoever' is changed to 'any place'	9.49	'and every sacrifice shall be salted with salt'
*6.11	'Verily I say…than for that city' [last part of the verse is omitted]	*10.21	'take up the cross'
		10.24	'for them that trust in riches'
		10.29	'or wife'
6.15	'or' [AV–'or as one of the prophets'; NAS –'like one of the prophets *of old*']	11.10	'in the name of the Lord'
		*11.11	'Jesus'
		*11.14	'Jesus'

Mark - Luke

*11.15	'Jesus'
11.24	'ye receive' is changed to 'you have received'
*11.26	ALL OF THIS VERSE IS OMITTED
12.4	'and at him they cast stones'
*12.30	'this *is* the first commandment'
12.33	'with all the soul'
*12.41	'Jesus'
13.8	'and troubles'
13.11	'neither do ye premeditate'
13.14	'spoken of by Daniel the prophet'
*13.33	'and pray'
14.19	'and another *said, Is* it I?'
*14.22	'Jesus'
*14.22	'eat' [AV–'Take, eat.' NAS –'Take *it*.']
*14.24	'new' ['of the new testament']
14.27	'because of me this night'
14.68	'and the cock crew'
14.70	'and thy speech agreeth *thereto*'
15.3	'but he answered nothing'
15.8	'crying aloud' is changed to 'went up'
*15.28	ALL OF THIS VERSE IS OMITTED
*15.39	'cried out'
16.8	'quickly'
*16.9-20	OMITTED or bracketed in most Bibles (with variations). Although missing in the Vatican and Sinai manuscripts, it is found in almost every Greek manuscript which contains Mark's Gospel. In addition it is quoted by Church Fathers including Irenaeus and Hippolytus in the second and third centuries (thus predating the two 'old' manuscripts, Vatican and Sinai).

LUKE

1.28	'blessed *art* thou among women'
1.29	'when she saw *him*'
2.5	'wife' [AV–'his espoused wife'; NAS–'who was engaged to him']
2.9	'lo'
*2.14	'good will toward men' is changed to 'toward men of good will' or 'among men with whom he is pleased'
2.17	'abroad'
*2.33	'And Joseph and his mother' is changed to 'and his father and mother' (note that the change affects the Virgin Birth of our Lord)
*2.40	'in spirit'
*2.43	'and Joseph and his mother' is changed to 'his parents' (cf. 2.33)
*4.4	'but by every word of God'
*4.8	'Get thee behind me, Satan: for'
4.18	'to heal the brokenhearted'
*4.41	'Christ' [first instance; the reference to Jesus' Messiahship is eliminated]
5.33	'why' [makes this a statement rather than a question]
5.38	'and both are preserved'
5.39	'straightway'
6.10	'whole as the other'
6.26	'unto you'
6.45	'treasure of his heart' [second instance]

6.48	'was founded upon a rock' is changed to 'had been well built'	11.54	'that they might accuse him'
		*12.31	'the kingdom of God' is changed to 'his kingdom'
7.10	'that had been sick'	*13.2	'Jesus'
*7.19	'Jesus'	13.19	'great'
*7.22	'Jesus'	13.35	'desolate' is in italics although it is in the Greek
7.31	'And the Lord said'		
*8.38	'Jesus'	13.35	'verily'
8.45	'and they that were with him'	14.5	'ass' is changed to 'son'
8.45	'and sayest thou, Who touched me?'	17.3	'against thee'
		17.9	'him? I trow [i.e., judge] not'
8.48	'be of good comfort'	*17.36	ALL OF THIS VERSE IS OMITTED
8.54	'put them all out, and'		
*9.43	'Jesus'	19.5	'and saw him'
9.50	'us' is changed to 'you'	20.5	'then'
9.54	'even as Elias did'	20.23	'Why tempt ye me?'
9.55	'and said, Ye know not what manner of spirit ye are of'	20.30	'took her to wife, and he died childless'
*9.56	'For the Son of man is not come to destroy men's lives, but to save *them*'	*21.4	'of God'
		21.8	'therefore'
		22.14	'twelve'
*9.60	'Jesus'	22.31	'And the Lord said'
10.1	'seventy' is changed to 'seventy-two'	*22.43	some versions omit ALL of this verse or put it in brackets
10.17	'seventy' is changed to 'seventy-two'	*22.44	some versions omit ALL of this verse or put it in brackets
10.20	'rather' [AV–'but rather'; NAS–'but']	*22.57	'him' [first instance] (referring to Jesus) is omitted or changed to 'it'
*10.21	'Jesus'		
10.35	'when he departed'		
*10.39	'Jesus' [Critical Text has 'Lord']	22.60	'the cock' is changed to 'a cock'
*10.41	'Jesus' [Critical Text has 'Lord']		
*11.2	'our' ['Our Father…']	*22.63	'Jesus'
*11.2	'which art in heaven'	22.64	'they struck him on the face, and'
*11.2	'Thy will be done, as in heaven, so in earth'		
		22.68	'also' [AV–'and if I also ask you, ye will not answer me'; NAS –'and if I ask a question, you will not answer']
*11.4	'but deliver us from evil'		
*11.11	'bread' and 'will he give him a stone? or if *he ask*'		
11.29	'the prophet'		
11.44	'scribes and Pharisees, hypocrites'	22.68	'nor let *me* go'
		23.6	'of Galilee' is changed to 'it' or omitted
11.54	'and seeking'		

*23.17	ALL OF THIS VERSE IS OMITTED	24.42	'and of an honeycomb'
23.23	'and of the chief priests'	24.49	'of Jerusalem'
23.25	'unto them'	24.51	'and carried up into heaven'. Only two Greek manuscripts omit this, but some Greek texts and critical editions of the Greek New Testament and some versions omit it.
*23.34	'Then said Jesus, Father, forgive them; for they know not what they do.' [some versions bracket this or have notes which say that this is not original]		
23.38	'written' and 'in letters of Greek, and Latin, and Hebrew'	*24.52	Some versions omit 'they worshiped him' from this verse for the same reasons as in the case of the omissions in 24.40; however, some critical editions of the Greek New Testament include it. Without it the risen Lord is not receiving worship from His people.
*23.42	'Lord' [the thief on the cross recognizes Jesus' Lordship]		
*23.43	'Jesus'		
*23.45	'And the sun was darkened' is changed to 'the sun being obscured', 'eclipsed' or 'failing', or a marginal reading is given to add this naturalistic effect.		
24.1	'and certain *others* with them'	24.53	'praising' is omitted from the critical Greek text; according to marginal note in NAS, NAS changes 'blessing' to 'praising'.
24.4	'much'		
*24.6	'He is not here, but is risen' is omitted from or bracketed in some versions, or a problematic footnote is given	24.53	'Amen'

JOHN

24.12	Some versions omit ALL of this verse, others only omit 'laid'
*24.36	'Jesus'
*24.40	Some versions omit or bracket this verse. It is found in every Greek manuscript of Luke except for one fifth century Western manuscript. The omission results from radical New Testament criticism principles. Some versions have misleading or incorrect footnotes regarding this.

*1.18	'only begotten Son' is changed to 'only begotten God'
1.27	'is preferred before me'
1.51	'Hereafter'
2.22	'unto them'
*3.2	'Jesus'
*3.13	'which is in heaven' [thus an attribute of God is removed from Jesus]
3.15	'should not perish, but' is omitted
*4.16	'Jesus'
*4.42	'the Christ' [note: Jesus' Messiahship is obscured]

A Textual Key to the New Testament

*4.46	'Jesus'	*9.4	'I must work the works' is changed to 'we must work the works'
5.3	'waiting for the moving of the water'		
*5.4	ALL OF THIS VERSE IS OMITTED	9.11	'the pool of'
		*9.35	'Son of God' is changed to 'Son of man'
5.16	'and sought to slay him'		
5.30	'Father'	10.26	'as I said unto you'
6.11	'to the disciples, and the disciples'	10.38	'believe' [third instance; AV–'know, and believe,'] is changed to 'understand' [NAS 'know and understand']
*6.14	'Jesus'		
6.22	AV–'save that one whereinto his disciples were entered' NAS –'except one'		
		11.41	*from the place* where the dead was laid'
6.39	'Father'	*11.45	'Jesus'
*6.47	'on me' [note: not just 'believing' secures everlasting life, but believing 'in me' (Jesus)]	12.1	'which had been dead'
		12.41	'when' is changed to 'because'
6.58	'manna'	13.2	AV–'And supper being ended'; NAS –'And during supper'
*6.69	'thou art the Christ, the Son of the living God' is changed to 'you are the Holy One of God' [note: Messiahship and Deity/Sonship are missing]		
		*13.3	'Jesus'
		14.12	'my' [NAS–'the Father']
		*14.15	'If ye love me, keep my commandments' (a command) is changed to a statement, 'If you love me, you will keep my commandments'
7.8	'yet'		
7.26	'very' ['this is the very Christ']		
7.29	'But'		
7.33	'unto them'		
*7.39	'Holy' ['Holy Ghost']		
*7.53-8.11	entire section is omitted or in brackets in many modern versions	14.28	'I said' [AV–'because I said, I go'; NAS –'because I go']
		15.7	'ye shall ask' is changed to 'ask'
8.9	'being convicted by *their own* conscience'	16.3	'unto you'
		16.10	'my' [NAS –'the Father']
*8.9	'Jesus'	*16.16	'because I go to the Father'
8.10	'and saw none but the woman'	17.11	'those whom' [referring to believers] is changed to 'that which' [referring to 'name']
8.10	'thine accusers'		
*8.16	AV–'the Father'; NAS–'He'		
*8.20	'Jesus'	17.12	'in the world'
*8.21	'Jesus'	*17.12	'I kept them in thy name: those that thou gavest me' is changed to 'I was keeping
8.59	'going through the midst of them, and so passed by'		

8

	them in Thy name which Thou hast given me;'	6.3	'Holy' [AV –'Holy Ghost'; NAS –'Spirit']
17.20	'shall' [AV–'which shall believe'; NAS –'who believe']	6.13	'blasphemous'
		*7.30	'of the Lord'
*18.5	'Jesus' [second instance]	7.37	'the Lord your'
19.16	'and led *him* away'	7.37	'him ye shall hear'
*19.38	'Jesus' [third instance]	*8.37	ALL OF THIS VERSE IS OMITTED
*19.39	'Jesus'		
20.19	'assembled'	9.5	'*It is* hard for thee to kick against the pricks'
20.29	'Thomas' [AV–'Jesus saith unto him, Thomas']		
		9.6	'And he trembling…unto him'
21.3	'immediately'		
		*9.20	'Christ' is changed to 'Jesus'
		*9.29	'Jesus' [part of verse 28 in the Critical Text]

ACTS

1.14	'and supplication'	10.6	'He shall tell thee what thou oughtest to do'
2.1	'with one accord' is changed to 'together'		
		10.21	'which were sent unto him from Cornelius'
2.7	'one to another'		
2.23	'have taken'	10.32	'who, when he cometh, shall speak unto thee'
*2.30	'according to the flesh, he would raise up Christ'		
		*15.11	'Christ'
2.33	'now'	15.18	AV–'Known unto God are all his works from the beginning of the world'; NAS–'who makes these things known from of old'
2.41	'gladly'		
2.42	'and' ['and in breaking of bread']		
*2.47	'to the church' is changed to 'to their number'	15.24	'saying, *Ye must* be circumcised and keep the law'
3.6	'rise up and'		
3.20	'Jesus Christ, which before was preached unto you' is changed to 'Jesus, the Christ appointed for you'	*15.34	ALL OF THIS VERSE IS OMITTED
		*16.31	'Christ'
		17.5	'which believed not'
3.24	'foretold' is changed to 'announced'	17.26	'blood'
		18.21	'I must by all means keep this feast that cometh in Jerusalem'
*3.26	'Jesus'		
4.24	'God'		
5.23	'without' ['the keepers standing without']	*19.4	'Christ'
		*19.10	'Jesus'
5.24	'the high priest, and'	*20.21	'Christ'
5.25	'saying'	*20.25	'of God' ['kingdom of God']
5.34	'apostles'	20.32	'brethren'

A Textual Key to the New Testament

20.34	'Yea'
21.8	'that were of Paul's company'
21.25	'that they observe no such thing, save'
22.9	'and were afraid'
22.16	'the name of the Lord' is changed to 'His name'
22.20	'unto his death'
23.9	'let us not fight against God'
23.15	'to morrow'
*24.6-8	'and would have judged…commanding his accusers to come unto thee' is omitted [the last part of verse 6, ALL of verse 7, and the first part of verse 8]
24.15	'of the dead'
24.26	'that he might loose him'
25.16	'to die'
26.30	'when he had thus spoken'
28.16	'the centurion delivered the prisoners to the captain of the guard: but'
*28.29	ALL OF THIS VERSE IS OMITTED

ROMANS

*1.16	'of Christ' ['the gospel of Christ']
1.29	'fornication'
1.31	'implacable ['unforgiving']
3.22	'and upon all'
5.2	a few versions omit 'by faith'
6.11	'our Lord'
*8.1	'who walk not after the flesh, but after the Spirit'
*8.26	'for us' [regarding the Holy Spirit's intercession] is omitted or italicized in some versions
8.28	AV–'all things work together for good'; NAS–'God causes all things to work together for good'
9.28	'in righteousness: because a short work' is omitted, and many versions rearrange what parts of the verse remain.
9.31	'of righteousness' [second instance]
9.32	'of the law'
10.1	'Israel'
*10.15	'preach the gospel of peace,'
*10.17	'God' is changed to 'Christ'
11.6	'But if *it be* of works, then is it no more grace: otherwise work is no more work'
*13.9	'Thou shalt not bear false witness'
14.6	'and he that…doth not regard *it*' [some versions omit this, some place it in brackets]
*14.9	'and rose'
*14.10	'Christ' is changed to 'God' [note: if 'Christ' is read in verse 10, then He is the God of verse 12. If the reading in verse 10 is 'God', then the Deity of Christ is missing in this passage]
14.21	'or is offended, or is made weak'
14.22	'Hast thou faith?' is changed from a question to a statement, 'the faith which you have'
*15.8	'Jesus'
15.24	'I will come to you'
*15.29	'of the gospel' ['of the gospel of Christ']
*16.18	'Jesus' ['Lord Jesus Christ']
*16.20	'Christ'

*16.24   ALL OF THIS VERSE IS OMITTED

1 CORINTHIANS

1.14	in some versions 'I thank God' is changed to 'I am thankful'
2.4	'man's'
*2.13	'Holy' is omitted from 'Ghost'
5.1	'named'
*5.4	'Christ' is omitted twice
*5.5	'Jesus' is omitted from some versions
*5.7	'for us'
*6.20	'and in your spirit, which are God's'
7.5	'fasting and'
7.39	'by the law'
*9.1	'Christ'
*9.18	'of Christ'
9.22	'as' ['became I as weak']
*10.9	'Christ' is changed to 'the Lord'
10.11	'all' ['Now all these things']
10.23	'for me' ['lawful for me']
10.28	'for the earth is the Lord's, and the fulness thereof'
*11.24	'Take, eat' [speaking of the Lord's Supper]
*11.24	'broken' [speaking of Christ's body]
*11.29	'unworthily'
*11.29	'Lord's' ['the Lord's body']
12.13	'into' ['into one Spirit'] is changed to 'of'
14.25	'And thus'
14.34	'your' ['your women']
14.38	'let him be ignorant' is changed from an exhortation to the statement, 'he is not recognised'
*15.47	'the Lord' [the Deity of Christ is obscured]
15.55	AV–'O death, where is thy sting? O grave, where is thy victory?'; NAS –'O death, where is your victory? O death, where is your sting?'
*16.22	'Jesus Christ'
*16.23	'Christ'

2 CORINTHIANS

1.10	'doth deliver' (second instance) is changed to 'shall deliver' in some versions; thus 'delivered...doth deliver...will yet deliver' becomes 'delivered...will deliver...will yet deliver'.
*4.6	'Jesus'
*4.10	'the Lord'
*5.18	'Jesus'
8.4	'that we would receive'
8.24	'and' ['and before the churches']
9.10	AV–'Now he...minister...and multiply...and increase'; NAS –'Now He...will supply and multiply...and increase', changing an expressed wish or prayer (voluntative optative) to a statement of future
*10.7	'Christ' [third instance]
10.8	'us' ['hath given us for edification']
11.6	'been' [AV–'we have been throughly made manifest'; NAS –'we have made this evident']
*11.31	'our'

*11.31 'Christ'
12.11 'in glorying'
13.2 'I write'

GALATIANS

*1.15 'God' is changed to 'He'
3.1 'that ye should not obey the truth'
3.1 'among you'
*3.17 'in Christ' [the Abrahamic covenant was 'in Christ']
4.7 'of God through Christ' is changed to 'through God'
4.24 'the' ['the two covenants']
5.19 'Adultery'
5.21 'murders'
*6.15 'in Christ Jesus'
*6.17 'the Lord'

EPHESIANS

1.10 'both'
1.18 'understanding' is changed to 'heart'
*3.9 'by Jesus Christ'
*3.14 'of our Lord Jesus Christ'
4.6 'you' ['in you all']
4.9 'first' ['he also descended first']
4.17 'other' ['other Gentiles'] is changed to 'the'
*5.9 'fruit of the Spirit' is changed to 'fruit of the light'
5.21 'fear of God' is changed to 'fear of Christ'
5.30 'of his flesh, and of his bones'
6.10 'my brethren'

PHILIPPIANS

1.16-17 these verses are reversed in the modern versions
3.3 'God in the spirit' is changed to 'in the Spirit of God'
*3.16 'let us mind the same thing'
*4.13 'Christ which strengtheneth me' is changed to 'him who strengthens me'
4.23 *be* with you all' is changed to 'be with your spirit'

COLOSSIANS

*1.2 'and the Lord Jesus Christ'
*1.14 'through his blood'
*1.28 'Jesus'
2.2 'and of the Father, and of'
2.7 'therein'
2.11 'of the sins of'
*2.18 'not' ['hath not seen' is changed to 'has seen']
2.20 'Wherefore'
*3.6 'on the children of disobedience'
*3.13 'Christ' is changed to 'the Lord'
*3.15 'God' is changed to 'Christ'
*3.22 'God' is changed to 'the Lord'
3.24 'for' is omitted, changing the conclusion of the Apostle's statement to a separate statement

1 THESSALONIANS

*1.1 'from God our Father, and the Lord Jesus Christ'
2.2 'even' ['But even after']

Galatians - Hebrews

*2.19	'Christ'
3.2	'minister'
*3.11	'Christ' [AV–'our Lord Jesus Christ'; NAS –'Jesus our Lord']
*3.13	'Christ'
5.27	'holy' ['holy brethren']

2 THESSALONIANS

*1.8	'Christ'
*1.12	'Christ' [first instance]
*2.2	'day of Christ' is changed to 'day of the Lord'
*2.4	'as God' [AV–'he as God sitteth'; NAS –'he takes his seat']

1 TIMOTHY

1.1	'Lord'
*1.17	'wise' ['only wise God']
*2.7	'in Christ' ['I speak the truth in Christ']
3.3	'not greedy of filthy lucre'
*3.16	'God' is replaced with 'he', 'he who', or 'what' (see the Society's Article no. 103, *God was Manifest in the Flesh*, regarding this passage)
4.12	'in spirit'
5.4	'good and'
5.16	'man or' [Greek: 'believing *man* or believing *woman*']
*6.5	'from such withdraw thyself'
6.7	'*and it is* certain'

2 TIMOTHY

1.1	'an apostle of Jesus Christ' is changed to 'an apostle of Christ Jesus'
1.11	'of the Gentiles'
*2.19	'name of Christ' is changed to 'name of the Lord'
4.1	'therefore'
*4.1	'Lord'
*4.22	'Jesus Christ'

TITUS

1.4	'mercy'
*1.4	'Lord' is omitted, and 'Jesus Christ' is reversed
2.7	'sincerity'

PHILEMON

*6	'Jesus'
*12	'Whom I have sent again: thou therefore receive him, that is, mine own bowels' is changed to 'And I have sent him back to you in person, that is, *sending* my very heart'

HEBREWS

*1.3	'by himself'
*1.3	'our' ['purged our sins']
*2.7	'and didst set him over the works of thy hands' is omitted in many versions
*3.1	'Christ'
3.6	'firm unto the end' is omitted in many versions
6.10	'labour of'
*7.21	'after the order of Melchisedec'
8.12	'and their iniquities'
*10.9	'O God' is omitted in many versions
*10.30	'saith the Lord'

10.34	'my' ['my bonds']	*1.22	'through the Spirit'
10.34	'in heaven'	1.23	'for ever'
*11.11	'was delivered of a child'. Some modern versions add, with no Greek manuscript support, an entire section about Abraham being enabled to beget children.	*3.15	'God' is changed to 'Christ'
		*4.1	'for us' ['Christ hath suffered for us']
		4.14	'on their part he is evil spoken of, but on your part he is glorified'
*11.13	'were persuaded of *them*'	5.8	'because'
*11.37	'were tempted' is omitted from most versions	*5.10	'Jesus'
		5.11	'glory and'
12.20	'or thrust through with a dart'	*5.14	'Jesus. Amen.'

JAMES

2 PETER

1.19	'Wherefore' is changed to 'this you know' and 'but' is added ['But let every one']	*1.21	'holy' ['holy men of God']
		2.17	'for ever'
		3.9	'us' is changed to 'you'
1.26	'among you'	3.10	'in the night'
2.18	'thy' [AV–'without thy works'; NAS–'without the works']	*3.10	'shall be burned up' is changed to 'discovered'; some versions have this change as a footnote only
2.18	'my' is omitted from most versions		
*2.20	'faith without works is dead' is changed to 'faith without works is useless'		

1 JOHN

4.2	'yet' [in addition to this omission, the NAS adds '*so*', giving the impression of causal relationship]	*1.7	'Christ'
		2.7	'brethren' is changed to 'beloved'
		2.7	'from the beginning' [second instance]
*4.4	'adulterers and'		
5.5	'as' ['as in a day of slaughter']	*2.20	'ye know all things' is changed to 'you all know'
5.16	'faults' is changed to 'sins' [different Greek words]	3.1	'and we are' is added after 'sons of God'
*5.20	'a soul' is changed to 'his soul'	3.14	'*his* brother' ['loveth not *his* brother']

1 PETER

1.16	'Be ye holy' [a command] is changed to 'you shall be holy' [future tense]	*3.19	'we know' is changed to 'we shall know' (but note the context)
		*4.3	'Christ is come in the flesh'

14

*4.19	'we love him' is changed to 'we love'	1.8	'the beginning and the ending'
*5.7-8	'in heaven; the Father, the Word, and the Holy Ghost: and these three are one. And there are three that bear witness in earth,' (See the Society's Article no. 102, *Why 1 John 5.7-8 is in the Bible.*)	*1.9	'Christ' is omitted twice
		*1.11	'I am the Alpha and Omega, the first and the last and'
		1.11	'which are in Asia'
		1.17	'unto me'
		1.20	'which thou sawest' [second instance]
*5.13	'and that ye may believe on the name of the Son of God'	2.9	'works'
		2.13	'thy works, and'
		2.15	'which thing I hate'
		3.4	'even' ['even in Sardis']

2 JOHN

		3.11	'Behold'
		5.4	'and to read'
		5.5	'to loose'
3	'the Lord'	5.6	'and, lo,'
9	'of Christ' [second instance]	5.14	'four *and* twenty'
		*5.14	'him that liveth for ever and ever'

3 JOHN

		*6.1,3,5,7	'and see' ['Come and see']
		6.12	'lo'
11	'but' ['but he that doeth evil']	*7.5b-8b	'*were* sealed' is omitted in ten of the twelve instances

JUDE

		*8.13	'I heard an angel' is changed to 'I heard an eagle'
		10.4	'unto me'
* 1	'sanctified' is changed to 'beloved'	*11.1	AV–'and the angel stood, saying'; NAS–'and someone said' (RSV 'and I was told')
* 4	'God'		
23	AV–'And others save with fear,' NAS–'save others,…and on some have mercy with fear'	11.4	'the God' is changed to 'the Lord'
		*11.17	'and art to come'
		12.12	'the inhabiters'
* 25	'wise' ['only wise God']	*12.17	'Christ'
25	some versions add 'before all time and'	*14.5	'before the throne of God'
		14.8	'city'
		14.12	'here *are* they'

REVELATION

		14.13	'unto me'
		14.15	'for thee'
		15.2	'over his mark'
*1.5	'loved us, and washed us' is changed to 'loves us and released us'	15.3	'the saints' is changed to 'the nations'
		15.5	'behold'

A Textual Key to the New Testament

*16.5	'O Lord'		'before the throne'
16.7	'another out of' [without this, an inanimate object, the altar, is speaking]	21.2	'John'
		21.5	'unto me'
		21.9	'unto me'
16.14	'of the earth and'	21.10	AV–'that great city, the holy Jerusalem'; NAS–'the holy city, Jerusalem'
16.17	'of heaven'		
17.1	'unto me'		
18.2	AV–'cried mightily with a strong voice'; NAS–'cried out with a mighty voice'	21.24	'of them which are saved'
		22.1	'pure'
		*22.14	'do his commandments' is changed to 'wash their robes'
18.6	'you' ['rewarded you']		
*19.1	'the Lord'	*22.19	'book of life' is changed to 'tree of life'
*20.9	'God out of'		
*20.12	'before God' is changed to	*22.21	'Christ'

NUMBER OF VARIANTS

Gospels	335
Acts	59
Pauline Epis.	142
Hebrews	16
General Epis.	44
Revelation	54
Total	**650**